PSYCHOANALYZING THE TWELVE ZODIACAL TYPES

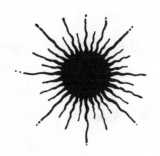

By

MANLY PALMER HALL

Fifth Edition

Martino Fine Books
Eastford, CT
2022

Martino Fine Books
P.O. Box 913,
Eastford, CT 06242 USA

ISBN 978-1-68422-669-6

Copyright 2022

Martino Fine Books

Cover Design Tiziana Matarazzo

Printed in the United States of America On 100% Acid-Free Paper

PSYCHOANALYZING THE TWELVE ZODIACAL TYPES

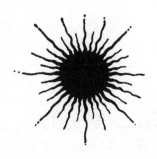

By

MANLY PALMER HALL

Fifth Edition

THE PHILOSOPHICAL RESEARCH SOCIETY, INC.
3341 GRIFFITH PARK BOULEVARD,
LOS ANGELES 27, CALIF.

CONTENTS

NOTE—*The Sun does not always pass into the new sign on the same day of the month. The 20th is approximate, but the proper ephemeris should be consulted for the exact time of ingress.*

THE CARDINAL SIGNS

♈ ♋ ♎ ♑

PART ONE

It is difficult to find a single keyword for the cardinal sign types. The term aggressive might seem appropriate, but examination and experience disclose too many exceptions. Perhaps the term persistent would be better, but it lacks fullness.

It is safe however to declare that most cardinal sign persons are self-centered, personality and purpose often hopelessly confused. It has not been my experience that cardinal sign types are as ambitious as fixed sign types, but contrary to the popular conception they are gifted with much persistency. Persistency is not always a synonym for consistency. Cardinal sign persons may change methods but they cling tenaciously to and struggle valiantly toward such goals as they set for themselves.

In attempting to analyze cardinal sign persons the word gratification seems to stand out. Most of these folk seem to be struggling desperately to satisfy themselves. Their own desires loom large on their mental horizons with the frequent result that they become indifferent to the rights and needs of others. They are not ruthless, but rather self-centered to the degree that they may be oblivious to the fundamental responsibilities and relationships of social existence.

Textbooks on astrology usually tell us that all cardinal sign people are born with the executive instinct, that leadership is not easy but necessary to them and that in menial positions or when bound to drudgery or routine they are among the most dissatisfied of mortals. We may as well say of all men that it is the natural desire of every normal human creature to excel. But no man can accomplish greatly without effort, without sacrifice and dedication. It frequently appears that cardinal sign persons have more of dedication to their purpose than the natives of less energetic signs. This may bring leadership but the rule is not invariable. Millions of cardinal sign folk are in menial positions, denied that superior place their egos long for. We may say that cardinal signs bestow *capacity* for leadership, but only their industry and enlightened effort can fill that capacity with the substance of greatness.

(4)

Let us then consider briefly the four cardinal sign types, attempting to discover something of the motivating power behind each and the temperamental peculiarities that distinguish them:

♈

ARIES

(*Those born March* 21—*April* 19)

There is something of the inevitable about the life and thought of the Aries people. There is indomitable purpose behind them. They are seldom defeated because they will not recognize defeat. Supplied normally with abundant energy, powerful constitution, and considerable personal courage, they are prepared for effort and strife and will ultimately win the goal they strive for unless a certain mental narrowness stands in their way.

Being under the rulership of the planet Mars, this sign is imbued with all that we call martial, and expresses its energy in constructive progress or destructive conquest according to type.

In the Aries type intellectual egotism is frequently present. They are sometimes too sure of themselves and are so prone to dominate situations that they often alienate the very persons most useful to them. It is a virtue to be sure of what one is; it is not always a virtue to be overly sure of what one knows, much less what one has.

Aries men may be cast in heroic molds, but heroics are less seemly in the feminine. The result is that the Aries woman is not likely to be the happiest of her sex. A home in which there is an Aries wife is apt to have two heads, a monstrosity unless both parties have reached a high degree of self-control. The Aries woman is an individualist, and unless her life is softened by the presence of more feminine signs or assisted by gentle planets she should look to a career rather than the home for the satisfaction of her ambitions.

The Aries man is fitted for pioneering and unusual endeavor. He is apt to think of his rewards in terms of fame rather than wealth, and he is generally satisfied and at his best as the not too modest recipient of adulation. His brow is shaped for laurels and his hairline is apt to recede in early life to make room for them.

Being strong, vital, and dynamic, he generally chooses in marriage a distinctly feminine type of woman. He is likely to find unhappiness if he marries the intellectual type of woman who chafes his ego. He is generally fond of children, either entirely spoiling them or feeling it his paternal duty to make for them all the major decisions of their life. Strangely enough, his home is frequently childless or he has few children, and they are not of very strong constitution. He is more apt to have daughters than sons.

Many of our astrological keywords have descended from a remote past when vocations and opportunities in life were vastly different from those afforded in our present social order. Therefore it does not necessarily follow that the military profession will be chosen by the modern Aries man. In an age where peace is regarded as more desirable than war, the Aries temperament frequently goes into the crafts and sciences and even the professions. The fighting instinct, however, survives. The Aries man is most likely to choose a life work which offers hazards and obstacles. He is not a natural desk man nor a time-clock puncher, and if he is pressed by necessity to such tasks his heart yearns for open places, for the glories and excitement of adventure.

The background of the Aries man is frequently one of adversity and struggle. His childhood is usually unhappy, and early in life these people must start out for themselves.

The result is an early development of resourcefulness and individuality. It is also common to find these persons self-educated. Working against numerous exigencies they fight their way toward the dignities and honors which are ever in their mind's eye.

Such men and women develop traits of opinionism and false sufficiency in self-defense. Experience does not fit them for the contemplative life, nor does it convince them of the intrinsic goodness of mankind. Their code may become the survival of the fittest, and their deepest comfort the realization that they are fit.

It would not be true to say that they are without human instincts. Their whole lives may be dedicated to pursuits which have as their final end the improvement or education of mankind. They are active fighters and for the most part have a high standard of integrity. If the Aries people can subdue the eruptive urges within, and can balance effort with reflection, they can become and have become some of the noblest instruments toward progress which the world produces out of its own necessity.

CANCER

(Those born June 21—July 22)

Although still definitely a cardinal type, the Cancer native is widely different in every part of his being from the person born under Aries. The most dominant factor that binds the two signs together is their self-centeredness. But in the Cancer type this egoism is far less organized and infinitely more fretful.

The difference between the two signs is well symbolized by the difference between the fiery Mars which rules Aries and the watery Moon which rules Cancer. The cardinal energy of Aries is like the sword-thrust, and the cardinal strength of Cancer is like the inevitable slow rise of the tide.

Of all the zodiacal types the Cancer child is most likely to be spoiled. Especially is this true of the boy who may grow up surrounded by the protection and sacrifice of a doting parent or relative.

Taken all in all, Cancer is a far more fortunate sign for women than for men. It is naturally a feminine sign dominated by feminine psychology and feminine emotions, and a man born under it must fight against not only effeminacy but a general weakness of character. This does not necessarily mean that a Cancer man cannot accomplish the finest and highest things in life, but it does generally mean that he must first overcome many things in himself if he is to accomplish them. Most of all, he must overcome emotional and moral weakness. He must struggle to gain control over the power to say Yes and No and mean it—Yes at the right time, and No at the right time.

The Cancer man frequently develops in childhood considerable personal vanity. In some cases this vanity may prove an inspiration to high accomplishment, but too frequently it leads only to dissatisfaction and fretfulness. The Cancer man is not always a fashion-plate, but many times he wears his whole fortune on his back. He must learn early that distinction comes not from tailoring but from thinking.

Vanity comes frequently from spoiling in childhood, from indulgence on the part of parents, and even from an injudicious sparing of the rod. Out of a considerable number of charts we have observed that Cancer children are frequently deprived of their fathers either through death or divorce, and it is a psychologically established fact that the loss of a parent or the failure of both parents to share in the upbringing leaves a definite mark on the child's character.

Cancer persons are usually very ambitious, not so much for the accumulation of wealth as for the gratification of their desire for luxury and their innate impulse to show outwardly the evidences of a strength of character which they frequently lack inwardly. Like most cardinal sign people Cancer is extremely ambitious in youth, but being somewhat easily disillusioned and easily demoralized, often sinks to comparatively insignificant position in advancing years. They fail to live up to early promise.

Psychologically, the Cancer man is supersensitive, shy, reticent and even negative. This condition is also aggravated by shielding, protecting, and petting in early life, but may be innate where the early life is not so pampered. Much of the vanity, indirectness, glibness, and "show-off" "big-front" tendencies of the Cancer man can be attributed to this almost abnormal sensitiveness. The crab has a protective shell because he is a very shy creature.

Cancer is the most psychic of the signs, and, being closely associated with the element of water, the most mutable of the elements, takes like water its form from its environment, often to its detriment. Like the chameleon, which is ruled by the sign, the Cancer man changes his colors to match his background. It is particularly unfortunate therefore if he mingles with undesirable associates who may stimulate in him his natural tendency to intemperance. Cancer men are kind, generous, optimistic, well-meaning, with a natural antipathy to responsibility, and they must take a strong grip on themselves and face life honestly and frankly if they expect to be happy.

The Cancer type makes a bad husband but a good wife. Assisted by stronger signs and better planetary placements, and strengthened by a strong resolve, a Cancer man can achieve to high position. But to reach this goal he must conquer the vacillation and uncertainty in himself. The Cancer man is fond of adventure and excitement, and is at his best when the center of an admiring throng, especially of the fair sex. He is usually successful in some line which contacts people and supplies needs in essential industries. He loves to travel, follow the sea for a profession, deal in liquids or fluids, and often shines in real estate.

The Cancer woman is often called the perfect mother and is usually of the gentle and benign type, but is subject to spells of melancholy or hysteria. Her mood changes with the Moon. There are large Cancer types, and small. The smaller types with dark eyes and hair have much quicker tempers and are frequently found in the teaching profession. Cancer women are prominent in education, nursing, kindergarten and social service work.

Both men and women find the theatre a fertile field of effort. Many of the popular leading men of stage and screen, of handsome profile, are born under Cancer.

We could say many nice things about Cancer folk, but this would not be as useful to them as a rather blunt exposition of their problems.

⚎

LIBRA

(Those born September 23—October 23)

Those born under Libra can read the description of Cancer with benefit, for in some respects their problems parallel. The Libra man usually succeeds in the field of the arts. His whole nature is emotional but by no means as intrinsically negative as is Cancer. His character is frequently built on early struggle. He is not usually one of those unfortunates born with a silver spoon in his mouth. Like Cancer, Libra is not a fortunate sign for a man to be born under, for it is the positive sign of the planet Venus, bestowing a little more than might be desirable of the feminine, of romance, love of luxury, and even of intemperance.

There are two distinct types of Libra men. The tall and slender type to which the arts of painting, sculpture and drawing are more common, and the somewhat heavier and more expressive type which finds the theatre, the concert hall, and even the circus to its liking. Salesmanship is close to drama, and when salesmanship and drama meet in the Libran, the result is apt to be a promoter.

There is a certain type of man who is sometimes referred to as a nagging old lady, and any Libra man should be very careful that it doesn't describe him. There is a natural streak of fault-finding and dissatisfaction in these people. They also have quick tempers, are ardent in their friendships and attachments, but not very enduring in their relationships. Multiple marriage is very frequent to Libra men, and strangely enough there are many cases where Libra men have married to spite someone.

Being one of the zodiac's most artistic signs, the Libra person is temperamental. The Libra artist is always criticising his critics and

(14)

wondering why his genius has not been discovered, and the Libra actor is apt to be at constant sword's point with his managers and his booking agents.

A curious Libran trait is the disease complex. They are definitely afraid of pain and at the slightest symptom of distress fear that the affliction is mortal. The appendix is a favored center of attention, but in spite of numerous fears it generally remains in place to the end of life.

Libra, when combined with Scorpio, Taurus or Leo, has exhibited extraordinary ambition, and in some cases great power of leadership. Libra was powerful in the nativities of Alexander the Great, Napoleon Bonaparte and Mahatma Gandhi. In all three cases these men, though of different aims, possessed in common great dramatic power —the ability to sway masses of people so that in the end their very words became laws. Adolph Hitler, with a powerful Libra ascending, brought the theatrical to the State in an astonishing exhibition of personal magnetism, swaying the usually sober and conservative Teutonic mind to his ends.

The Libra person loves to influence people, to feel that he has the power to mold the emotions of others. Like Hitler, the appeal of Sarah Bernhardt, also a Libran, was largely personal.

Recognizing this quality, it is most important that the Libra person build into his life so high a character and so noble a resolve that he will not be tempted to use his influence for improper or unworthy ends.

Like all of the cardinal signs, Libra is very conscious of rewards. He demands more of applause, however, than of wealth or fame. His picture in the newspaper means a great deal to him, and he may sacrifice too much to get it there. The publicity complex is seldom consistent with peace of mind or domestic happiness. He is born under a sign that predisposes him to criticism, scandal, and lawsuits, and only an exemplary life will protect him from notoriety.

Of course the average Libran will not rise to dictatorial spheres, but he can bring them down to himself and even in an obscure life can exhibit the same tendencies and dispositions that are apparent in those better publicized.

The Libra man should avoid mannerisms and cultivated peculiarities. He should avoid effeminacy, and as far as possible bring his emotions under the guidance of his reason.

Libra women share the artistic and esthetic abilities of the men, are generally of prepossessing appearance with finely organized features and attractive personalities. They will have less disturbance and unrest, less of fear and foreboding than the men, but even in their domestic life will be somewhat given to theatrics. Many Libra women in business, if not in drama or music, deal in cosmetics, hairdressing, clothes designing, and interior decorating. This sign also produces men who follow these professions.

VS

CAPRICORN

(Those born December 22—January 19)

Saturn, the ruler of the latter part of life, according to the ancients, is enthroned in Capricorn and turns the minds of those born under it distinctly toward the end of things. As soon as Capricorn persons are old enough to worry, and they begin early, they start worrying about security. They have a deadly fear of dependence, and because fear is a negative and destructive force they frequently fear themselves into a state of dependency.

Capricorn is kinder to men than to women, or rather it might be more proper to say it presents a greater problem to women. Capricorn men are a provident type, long-living, frequently successful in the last third of life. Capricorn women, being likewise long-lived, frequently outlive their husbands and face long years of aloneness which they are incapable of filling with useful and constructive thoughts and acts. Instead of viewing aloneness as freedom and the privilege of living one's own life, they view it as loneliness and isolation, and by their very melancholy become unwelcome to their friends and relatives.

Usually the Capricornian problem hinges on money, and there is no place where the problem of money hits harder. Of all the signs, fundamentally Capricorn has the highest and deepest ambitions, although these ambitions are less evident than in the more expressive signs. Capricorn is deeply introverted, and though longing to express itself has great difficulty in overcoming the rigidity and frigidity of its personality.

Capricornians are also among the most exacting of people. They are extremely critical of others and by their very criticism destroy many opportunities for companionship and affection. Unless fortune lifts them to a high place, and this of course is limited to the few, it is necessary for them to work out their problems within themselves and to discover peace and happiness through the relaxing of their own tension, and the cultivation of a gentle and charitable attitude toward others.

The egocentric is particularly expressive of Capricornians. Their whole perspective is bound up in themselves. Their own purposes assume cosmic proportions, and if they fail to attain their end they regard it as a cosmic disaster. The miseries and misfortunes of others are comparatively unimportant, but their own miseries and misfortunes, though frequently far less severe, are cataclysmic.

The real fact of the matter is, the average Capricornian does not know how to be happy. He has not discovered that the secret of happiness is to lose one's self in some effort to enlighten or make others happy, and not to constantly struggle for selfish comforts and security. The Capricornians are among the "sacrificing" people. As parents they are extremely possessive of their children and frequently remind them how much they have sacrificed for them. Until the Capricornian realizes that life is sacrifice and that to serve others is the greatest joy in life, only a very small amount of happiness can be his. Asking nothing, the universe gives us all; asking everything, the universe gives us nothing. We are rewarded not according to our desires but according to our merits.

As parents, Capricorn persons are frequently over-indulgent, not so much from a sense of real joy but because they regard it as a duty. The result is that many dissipate their possessions and come to a dependency which is neither necessary nor really helpful.

The Capricorn man has something about him that makes one think of a college professor. He may be a disciplinarian and hard-shelled, certainly a conservative, and rather impatient of the faults of the world. He is of that good, steady stock that in this day of volatility is likely to lose credit for its fundamental virtues because of the irascibilities of the disposition.

The one promising thing that may lift the shadow from many Capricorn lives is that nature is frequently kind to these people in the later part of life, giving them after sixty, more of peace and success than in early years.

In arts and sciences they are a thorough people, given to long and arduous labors which only in the end after many years bring their reward. In business they are likely to be too honest and thorough for prevailing standards, but in these matters it is better to please self than the world. Capricornians are suited to occupations such as bookkeepers, statisticians, mathematicians, students of ancient sciences and languages; Egyptology interests them and they are often collectors of antiquities. Sometimes they find their way into the clergy. They are thorough as teachers, prominent as superintendents and managers, and admirable in all places of trust. It is said that a business does well that has a Jupiterian for a developer and a Capricornian for a treasurer.

Capricorn people need to be busy, should avoid as much as possible association with the old, should dress and think with a realization that a person is really only as old as he feels. For this reason the Capricornian may be old at forty and young at eighty. Mental discipline and the cultivation of constructive, progressive ideas may result in a general rejuvenation of the whole life. When the Capricornian grows out of himself and gets, so to speak, his second wind, there is nothing he cannot accomplish. But first must come self-mastery.

THE FIXED SIGNS

♉ ♌ ♍ ♒

The fixed signs, Taurus, Leo, Scorpio, and Aquarius, bestow a peculiar tenacity of viewpoint which in exceptional cases contributes to greatness but more frequently creates the impression of stubbornness. There is an odd psychological twist in the mental processes of those dominated by fixed sign qualities. A misunderstanding world employs the terms "bull-headed," "opinionated" or "egocentric" to describe these people. In reality the fixed sign native may enjoy a very flexible, adjustable mentality, generous to a fault, willing and striving desperately to be helpful. Yet in spite of all these sincere endeavors to be constructively useful, disposition thwarts enterprise. Nor do fixed sign people really have bad dispositions in the general sense of the word. The only way we can explain it is to say that there is a blind spot in their mental processes, there is a delightful obliviousness often approaching *naivete* in their ability to overlook and ignore the elements in them-

(22)

selves that are working against success and happiness.

Whatever tendencies develop in the fixed sign nature they root deeply and cling tenaciously. It is very difficult for fixed sign persons to cure or overcome faults in themselves. In fact it is very hard for them to see their faults, and they frequently blame others for conditions which arise as the result of their own attitudes. It is perhaps difficult for the fixed sign native to analyze himself honestly. When he discovers his own faults, or others remind him of them he may become belligerent or at least extremely defensive. He will announce with an air of finality that people will have to take him the way he is or not at all. The result is that they probably do not take him at all. Of course people should not live to please others alone or to mold themselves into the whims of others, but a belligerent defense of aggravating traits of character is seldom profitable to anyone.

The relentlessness of fixed sign driving power, when directed to some definite purpose, is peculiarly suited to the building up of careers. The jack-of-all-trades is not common to fixed sign types. They are usually one-life-work people. They may attempt many different enterprises, but are only really successful and happy when they devote their energies to the one thing they have always wanted to do. Being somewhat inflexible due to this one dominating thought, they suffer emotionally and mentally when placed in situations contrary to their own purposes, adjusting only with difficulty.

Most fixed sign persons have a keen dramatic sense. They know how to dramatize what they are and what they do. Ability is seldom recognized unless the person possessing it possesses also a sense of dramatic values. Great generals such as Napoleon, Washington and Grant, dictators like Mussolini and Hitler, and leaders like Lincoln and Gandhi, are examples of men whose influence and prestige have been heightened by injecting dramatic values into their lives. In America there have been many fixed sign personalities in the drama of high finance such as the glamorous "Diamond Jim" Brady and the heads of the all-powerful House of Morgan. Religion, with its profoundly dramatic appeal, has contributed a large share of brilliant fixed sign personalities. The leaders of the majority of modern occult movements have had powerful Leo, Scorpio, and Aquarius placements in their nativities. There is no more dramatic personality than the humanitarian, and long-visioned humanitarianism is frequently a fixed sign quality.

All in all, the fixed sign native possesses the fixation of capacity and determination. By self-control and the refinement of his own nature he may add certain gentle, human qualities so that he will be loved rather than feared, respected rather than envied. It is a great gift to be gentle without being weak, to be kind and still strong, to lead without domineering, to command without tyranny. The fixed sign person seeking success must resolve in his own heart that he will not achieve at the expense of others, that he will transmute his fixation into a dedication, and will devote his life solely to purposes and ambitions that are constructive and progressive.

Of course the average fixed sign person will not come to great world prominence any more than the average person of any other group of signs, but in his own walk of life he will be concerned with the problem of comparative excellence and a certain urge to dominate situations no matter how small or great these situations may be. The struggle for accomplishment inevitably results in tension. A constant striving is a painful and often destructive process, destroying health and normalcy of viewpoint. Nearly all great persons have purchased success at the expense of happiness, poise, and health, and in the end are too invalided by the wear and tear of achieving to administer intelligently their success. Relaxation is absolutely necessary to health, happiness and efficiency. Fixed sign people must learn to "let go," "let down" and "let up." They must learn to play and enjoy communion with art, literature and esthetics. They must stop worrying over the magnitude of their affairs or the greatness of the responsibilities, develop a sense of humor and some of the Common Sign adjustability. They should not take themselves, their work, or the world so seriously that they lose perspective and the ability to enjoy the gentler and more temperate aspects of living.

ʘ

TAURUS

(Those born April 20—May 20)

Money is probably the dominating force in the life of the Taurean. It would not be correct to say that he is entirely devoted to a desire for wealth, but he is certainly an individual whose tastes can seldom be gratified without money. One type of the Taurean is the conventional business man whose life is largely devoted to buying and selling. He regards business as the principal justification for living and accepts a vacation as a necessary preparation for more intensive economic endeavor. Another type of Taurean is the financier represented principally by the banker and the stockbroker. These men take money very seriously, not necessarily because they have great quantities of it themselves, but because they are responsible for it. By constantly living in a world of money and money problems they come to think that the universe is co-ordinated principally through the monetary system. Many suicides over financial entanglements, losses and problems occur with this type. They may not be rich but they take money greatly to heart.

A third type of Taurean is the artist. In this group we can include all the degrees of artistic consciousness from the one who sells jewelry or millinery, to the esthete and the connoisseur of the fine arts; and all whose lives are devoted to some form of that intangible element which we term beauty or appropriateness in things. Again the economic factor is present. Art is the great luxury of the race. Luxury must be supported by wealth. The collector and the connoisseur must be a person of means in order to indulge his love of the beautiful.

Another type of Taurean is the performing artist. Here again the gamut is great, extending from the lowly Thespian making one night stands, to the great painter and sculptor whose masterpieces are of incalculable value. The interpretative and performing artist also includes the singer, the dancer, and to some extent the musician, although this sign is not so prominent among instrumentalists. Careers producing beauty or entertaining the world are also closely involved in economics. The motion-picture star is one of the most highly paid members of society, while the struggling artist in his garret is one of the poorest paid of human society, two extremes where money is an important factor. Art, except under the patronage of wealth, is one constant struggle against economic limitation, with small hope for fame until after death.

There is one other class of Taureans: the gardeners, horticulturists, and landscape artists. Many a Taurean of the financial or economic type finds release for his soul in building trellises for his sweet peas or carefully pruning his favorite rose bushes. It is natural and almost necessary for the Taurean to get close to the earth. The financier growing old will also build museums and art galleries to live after him in his community. Art and wealth are curiously related forces.

The average man or woman born under this sign must seek to balance the forces of his nature. He must soften with the love of beauty certain hard, driving elements of his thought, and if possible, with some actual participation in the arts. It will come naturally to him if he tries. The Taurean women in particular need artistic and esthetic expression to supply a natural Venusian vanity and a directed, purposeful expression of an intense emotional nature.

The Taurean man needs art for the sake of perspective. It is a sad thing to make money all one's life and not have an intelligent idea of how to spend it. The only thing that wealth can do for the individual is to give him an opportunity to improve himself and deepen his appreciation for all of the fine things of life. Most sucessful men are boors because they have given their lives to accumulation with no thought whatever to an intelligent and beautiful use of their money. The artist in his garret has little personal financial consciousness. The business man in his office has a very warped concept of the beauties of life. Each of these types instinctively, often unknowingly, yearns after that which it lacks —equilibrium—that force which is the true beauty of nature and is most necessary to happiness.

Thoughtfulness is an excellent virtue for Taureans to cultivate, and they need also a considerable measure of patience. Impatience frazzles nerves and nerves lead to misery. Each Taurean member of society in his or her own world should learn to enjoy the simple things, should cultivate the love of people and the love of humanity. It is not the intention to preach but rather to philosophize, and Taureans will do well to philosophize a little about the moods and forces within themselves. All artistic temperaments have a tendency to be temperamental and difficult. Temperament is just uncontrolled and undirected energy. A good disposition does not come from building it up but rather by directing energy into constructive and esthetic channels where it will contribute to the beauty of life and to the happiness of all men.

♌

LEO

(*Those born July 23—August 22*)

The Sun, ruler of Leo, is the symbol of the majesty of the solar system. The Sun, giver of life to all things, the sovereign spirit of the world, universal benefactor, bestows upon those ruled by it some aspect of its kingly quality and nature, and a desire to shine in this small world as the orb of day itself shines in the firmament. But the sun, though noble and benevolent, can shine too hotly and by its very light and warmth, in over-dose, parch and wither the earth, causing great deserts where heat becomes the constant enemy of life. Leo people of temperate nature are lights to the world, but if intemperate their glow turns into a withering glare. Light, like everything else in nature, must be controlled.

The psychology of Leo people is as compact and unified as that of the Taurean is diffused. The Leo temperament is made up of a combination of idealism and fatalism. As idealists they have a tendency to demand of society more of perfection and integrity than society is capable of producing. As fatalists nearly all Leo persons are struggling with the problem of destiny. They all want to do something or be something and if, as is frequently the case, they are not trained to do anything and have no particular purpose in life, they become irritable, dissatisfied and hypercritical.

Leo is a conservative sign, frequently prudish, easily offended and disillusioned in people and things, but with a highly developed sense of devotion to that which they have accepted as a standard of right or to persons exemplifying such a standard. Most Leo persons are strict individualists and they resent effort on the part of others to dominate their thinking or living. Especially is this true of Leo women who do not usually make good wives unless there is a feminine sign with it. Many Leo people go into educational fields, particularly religious or philosophical education. Also they are enthusiastic reformers, sacrificing health and even life to what they believe to be a great social purpose. They are naturally paternal in their attitude toward the world, viewing humanity as children who must be brought to a better condition whether they will or not.

Leo people are not consistently interested in wealth. Rather they desire approbation or recognition. To them money is desirable principally as a means of accomplishing personal independence. They may or may not be ambitious socially, but social climbing is not uncommon to Leo types when the sign is strengthened by a powerful placement of Mars or Jupiter.

Leo men succeed best in professions or positions of leadership, even though they direct the activity of only a few other persons. Although the sign is naturally ambitious in the sense of desiring preferment and advancement there is a certain type of Leo person almost entirely lacking in ambition or initiative, being perfectly willing to remain in a reasonably secure place and not desirous of assuming additional responsibilities or worries.

Leo, backed by another strong sign, is naturally dictatorial, autocratic, and with a fixed sign force behind it, even despotic. But always for a reason. The Leo person believes that the end justifies the means in whatever he is doing. The more aggressive type reforms people whether they want to be reformed or not, and frequently shows the divinity complex. A good example of this is Mussolini, who stated in a press conference that he could not be assassinated because Destiny had placed him there and Destiny would sustain him. What is this Destiny urge behind so many fixed sign people? In the majority of cases it is not a divine decree at all, but the terrific driving power inside of them, a certain kind of ambition combined with the temperament of an exhibitionist.

Leo men succeed admirably in certain types of promotion work, politics, religion, the civil service, as executives, and often in banking and monetary matters. They are frequently employed in large corporations, reaching the position of department heads, branch managers, foremen, and other positions of comparative authority where they have enough of responsibility and leadership to satisfy the seriousness of their natures. Responsibility is a special factor in their mental psychology. They are honest and true, often carrying heavy loads of responsibility through choice rather than necessity. They have a tendency to make much out of little in matters of responsibility, are thoroughly trustworthy unless the infallibility complex has unseated their common sense.

Under the divinity complex they mean to be honest but they bestow a certain infallibility upon their own thoughts which is not always justified by the grade of their intelligence. They take themselves very seriously and are completely demoralized by humiliation of any kind. To be demoted or even to retract a stated word or to be proved wrong is very hard for them. They do not take correction easily, but under certain exceptional conditions they will give great respect to the opinion of one whom they highly venerate.

The Leos are proud people and the grandeur complex is not by any means unknown to them. They enjoy the distinction of public office and can be depended upon for personal appearance. Gold braid, epaulets and medals mean much to them, and they have a peculiar veneration for superiority in tradition or position.

(34)

There is a peculiar faithfulness about the Leos in matters of trust. What they believe in they will serve to the end faithfully and unswervingly. For the most part they function in a narrow sphere of experience; broad outlooks are difficult for them, and they have great difficulty in outgrowing inadequacies of early life and education. Leos have a great capacity for accomplishment, but are very apt to devote themselves to a cause not worthy of them and to remain faithful to things that were better given up.

♏

SCORPIO

(Those born October 24—November 22)

Considering everything, Scorpio is probably the most difficult sign of the Zodiac to analyze briefly and comprehensively. Though rich in the driving energy of the fixed sign types, Scorpio is naturally introverted and the energy turned back upon itself produces an extraordinary diversity of chemical reactions. Possibly the principal fault of the Scorpio individual is his intensity of feeling, and the next most powerful factor is secretiveness. Intensiveness plus secretiveness result in an extremely complex and highly tense inner life.

(35)

It is very seldom that you find secretiveness without criticism and suspiciousness. These elements nearly always work together. Persons who lock a great deal inside of themselves judge others by themselves and over-estimate the inward workings of other persons' minds and feelings.

The Scorpio individual must start early in life to develop frankness and directness of thought and action. Every involved emotion or ulterior motive must be ferreted out by a strict analysis of self. Mars, as the ruler of Scorpio, gives a quick temper and a combative nature. Scorpio, being the night house of Mars, turns the Martial energy into the devious courses of jealousy and intrigue. The sharpness of Mars may also be present, but Scorpio persons very seldom engage in an active Martial occupation. The weapon of Aries is the sword, the weapon of Scorpio is the tongue. Scorpios have a way of putting a little sting into their remarks which arouses antagonism in others when such is not their intention. There are very few Scorpio persons who have come to a happy and normal condition of living who have not fought out the matter of their own temperaments and mastered certain difficult tendencies in themselves. Fortunately Scorpio also bestows the determination and will power to conquer, and these people *can* master themselves. When they have accomplished this by transmutation and not by brute force they are very useful and important people, capable of doing a great deal of good in this world. Everything in nature has compensation. The more difficult the accomplishment, the greater the reward, and to master a difficult disposition is one of the greatest of human accomplishments.

The professions of Scorpio follow the general inference of the sign. Secret agents, spies, detectives, inspectors of various kinds, and persons seeking hidden and obscure forms of knowledge all group together under this sign. Also under Scorpio come certain classes of scientists doing research work as in chemistry and bacteriology. Some surgeons, and a certain class of statisticians also come under the sign. It is further associated with the occult sciences. In the ancient Mysteries, initiation into the higher grades was usually given with the sun in Scorpio.

Because of its various qualities, the ancients devised several symbols to represent the sign. The lowest was the scorpion, the back-biter. Then came the serpent with its bitter tooth. Then the eagle with its strength of wing, and lastly the phoenix, bird of immortality and regeneration.

The average man or woman born under Scorpio is concerned principally with the effect of his disposition upon his business and his personal life. Successful men have discovered that one of the most important secrets of success is to eliminate the peculiarities of their own dispositions and temperaments which stand between them and their achievement. Mars is the bitter enemy of Venus according to the ancient astrologers, and Culpepper advised the astro-physicians of England to treat the diseases of Mars with the remedies of Venus upon the theory of antipathetical medicine. Now, the remedies of Venus include not only the herbs of the field but the arts and crafts of Venus. Most Scorpio persons are not interested in esthetics. They are much more apt to be of the mental type, wrestling intellectually with their dispositions as Jacob wrestled with the angel.

Beauty is the peculiar medicine of the soul, and in the presence of beauty and culture even the most tempestuous mind becomes silent with veneration. Music is an extremely valuable antidote for Scorpio tension because it bestows the element of rhythm to a life naturally choppy, erratic and angular. Of course in music the Scorpio individual should not indulge the morbidity or introversion that may be in his nature. Several great modern composers ruled by Scorpio have produced music which was worse than the malady it was intended to cure. Whatever Scorpio attempts it should simplify and render gentle, placid and flowing.

It is difficult to give a brief formula that will cover a wide diversity of issues, but recreation accompanied by relaxation and some natural healthy exercise of the body is of great virtue to all fixed sign people, especially to Scorpio. A sense of humor is a saving grace, but it is ruined if it becomes cynical or sarcastic. The great humorist laughs with the world, not at the world. Humor rendered entirely alkaline by a fundamentally good disposition is a free circulation of fresh air in a stuffy life. It should be especially cultivated in its round, jovial aspect, not hysterical but simple, evidencing the ability to see life not only as tragedy but as comedy. The realization that by a wise decree of Providence man is not in a position to do himself a great deal of harm no matter how hard he tries, would help Scorpio people to get the weight of the universe off themselves and back onto the shoulders of universal law. We do not mean that the Scorpio person should be flippant, but merely relaxed, for when strain is gone efficiency increases.

Like all the fixed signs, Scorpio must fight the tension problem. Being naturally introverted, this sign may develop the most acute forms of tension, even to the point of a nervous breakdown. Tension bottled up and given no free circulation offers a particularly difficult problem, affecting the general health and capable of precipitating chronic disease into the body.

These people have to be very careful how they react to things seen and heard. A natural suspiciousness may cause them to build into perfectly harmless circumstances causes of worry, irritation and dissatisfaction. Scorpio persons must rejoice in the good fortune of others, and make it their business in life to justify as far as they can the actions of others, trying definitely to see the other side of problems. By so doing they will lengthen their own lives and will come into the real wealth of the constructive aspect of the sign. Some of the world's greatest and noblest thinkers have been under Scorpio, for when their lives have been put in order and thoroughly disciplined they become capable and worthy of the role of teacher, guide and preceptor.

AQUARIUS

(Those born January 20—February 18)

The most volatile of the fixed signs is
Aquarius and it sometimes requires considerable examination to determine accurately the
fixation present in the erratic temperaments
of many natives born under this sign. There
are two distinct types of Aquarius—the Saturnine and the Uranian. The Saturnine
Aquarians have much more of the atmosphere
of the substantial about them. Their lives
are more ordered and their minds less flighty
and eccentric. The Uranian Aquarians seem
to be anchored to nothing. They defy all
efforts to organize them, and choose to be
free souls at the expense of worldly comforts
and in defiance of social traditions. Yet with
all their apparent scatteredness, Aquarians are
really quite fixed and definitely set in their
ways. It is as difficult to reform the scattered
notions of the Aquarian as it is to rearrange
the deep seated temperaments of other fixed
signs.

The Aquarian suffers from the habit of
chaos. He may not be anti-social but he is
certainly a nonconformist, greatly subject to
fads and innovations, and is a confirmed ex-

perimentalist. He generally succeeds best in some inventive pursuit. His gamut extends from being a handy man at the bottom of the ladder to being a great inventor like Thomas Edison at the top. Mechanically he is a natural tinkerer and fixer; socially the same, politically the same, religiously the same. The untrained Aquarian dislikes the arduous task of mastering a science or art. At the same time he would enjoy being regarded as an expert on almost any subject. Thus a keyword for him is dilettante. Too scattered to settle down and become proficient, he is apt to feel like the storied grasshopper who sang: "The world owes me a living!"

Unless the Aquarian is supported by some serious and organizing astrological factors he is not fitted for routine employment other than mechanics or aeronautics. He can, however, succeed admirably in some position involving travel, an outdoor or free-lance life without very close supervision, or in business for himself in some line which has the element of constant novelty. A great many astrologers come under this sign, including several very good ones. Astrology needs defending and championing at the present time, and Aquarians love to champion something. They get a great and sincere joy from helping along good causes, and they like to take part in all kinds of progressive, mildly revolutionary undertakings.

The Aquarian cannot help it if he is born in the objective case, nor can he help it apparently if he has to disagree with everyone else in the world. The thing he can do is to train himself to be different without being obnoxious. The average Aquarian is almost useless in a position requiring diplomacy or gentle and politic handling. In such a delicate position he generally succeeds in making everybody angry. Some good placements in gentler signs will modify this tendency, but even the most conservative Aquarian will finally be convicted of being some kind of ultra-progressive, an innovationist and an experimentalist.

Aquarian people are not generally very fortunate in matters of health. The natural constitutional diseases of the sign seem to be nervous disorders or tuberculosis, and frequently there is affliction to the ears or legs, which may add physical irritation to the nervous system, making a difficult temperament.

Aquarian women are apt to have domestic inharmonies, as they agitate easily and are subject to unstable moods. Like the men they are easily offended by anyone who differs with them, taking non-agreement as a personal insult. Aquarian women are also quite ambitious, rather vivacious, and have positive personalities. They generally dress well, and though not necessarily good looking, create an illusion of charm and beauty by good taste. They are nervous, tense people, and Aquarian women in business work under considerable tension and are greatly put out by trivial annoyances. Such traits as are undesirable should be worked upon with conscious effort and overcome. Most tense persons are irritable, and relaxation is again the indicated remedy.

Aquarian men will get along better in the world and put their ideas over more adequately if they will work on one idea at a time and present it non-pugnaciously. We can stimulate the world by insulting it, but, after all, to educate it by slow and gradual means is more permanent than merely to irritate it with a controversial attitude. Controversy and debate may be profitable and useful in moderation. In public life they succeed best upon directed policies with moderation as the watchword.

Aquarius produces many crisis leaders because the sign has vision and can bridge across from old to new things. The Aquarian visionary therefore must build a foundation under his vision and must equip himself to take a permanent place in the building of future civilization. His own unpreparedness is his greatest liability. If he can overcome this and master little fixations of attitude and notions, and the unpleasant peculiarities of his disposition, there is no end to what he can accomplish. He is usually crippled by a bad personality or at least one that does not present him in his best light. Routine, order and self-discipline—these are the medicines that his soul requires.

THE COMMON SIGNS

♊ ♍ ♐ ♓

PART THREE

The word "versatility" is frequently used as a collective keyword for common sign types. Necessity is properly called the mother of invention, and the ingenuity and resourcefulness of the common sign people bear witness, in the majority of cases, to these traits used in the struggle for survival. Common sign rulerships bestow difficult and arduous lives and success gained against great odds, attended with heavy responsibilities. Men born under common signs usually start out early

(45)

in life on courses of independent action. Education is gained with difficulty and economic issues are solved only with stress, if at all.

The common signs do not bestow the driving power of the cardinal types or the inflexibility of the fixed signs. There is likely to be less high ambition or intensive continuity. The secret of success for common signs is flexibility, nonresistance, thereby to adjust easily to life's often outrageous fortunes.

We can see that, taken collectively, common signs are intellectual rather than emotional, but the intellectuality is apt to be shallow or devoted to superficial subjects unless the horoscope includes emphasis of depth and thoroughness from other zodiacal or planetary placements.

The common signs are occasionally referred to as "terminal" and the houses most natural to these signs—the 3rd, 6th, 9th and 12th—are known as the terminal houses because they are most closely associated with the consummation or termination of life's various events and circumstances. Nearly all common sign persons come into the world bringing with them what may be termed "unfinished business." Life is a pattern of responsibilities, and their destiny seems to be constantly influenced by factors beyond personal control.

The common signs are collectively generous, unselfish and self-sacrificing, often with the worst implication of the self-sacrifice quality. The generosity of the common sign people is not always wisely administered, but the hardships of their own lives make them peculiarly sympathetic to the misfortunes of others. Sympathy is a good common sign keyword and is a quality which may be greatly exploited by unscrupulous relatives and acquaintances.

The common signs do not bestow either a hardy constitution or any unusual measure of will power. The vitality not being great, there is insufficient energy to sustain ambition or the urge to power. As a result, common sign folk predominate in menial capacities and in positions of obscurity. Family relationships are powerful with most common sign people. Though not consistently fortunate in marriage, these types are in great need of companionship, frequently centering their affection upon their children, idealizing and overshadowing their offspring to an uncomfortable, even dangerous, degree.

In matters of health the common signs incline to such infirmities as arise from lowered resistance and lack of body tone. The lack of resistance can be either mental or physical.

(47)

These people are subject to intemperances in eating and drinking and find great difficulty in mastering the appetites. Each of the common signs exhibits these qualities to a different degree, but the fundamental elements are present in all four signs. With the body resistance low, muscular tone poor, the respiratory and digestive functions are the most quickly attacked by disease or infirmity.

Unless subjected to constant discipline the mental processes of the common sign types are apt to be scattered or non-eventuating. There is a distinct tendency to carry along unfinished business and to procrastinate in decision. If left to its own disorder, the mind may deteriorate into a tumbling ground for whimsies. The mental disorder is frequently reflected in physical disorder and the common signs taken together are the least orderly of the zodiacal types. This trait may be overcome through training. One common sign thinker, apologizing for the chaotic condition of his study, explained that there was method in the madness, that he knew where everything was, and that the state of his belongings was a divine disorder.

♊

GEMINI

(*Those born May 21—June 20*)

Gemini is the most intellectual of the common signs, being the throne of the nervous, mental planet Mercury. The Gemini native is naturally fitted for walks of life requiring precision and exactness of the mental processes. It does not necessarily follow that the intellectual person is the deepest thinker or possesses the most capable reasoning powers. We must, therefore, in the case of the Gemini person, separate the intellect from the reason. The Mercurial thinker does not necessarily understand what he thinks about, but resembles the young college student whose head is filled with years of theory but who possesses practically no experience in the art of living or the science of understanding.

You will, therefore, most frequently contact Gemini people in some walk of life dealing with theoretics or basking in the aura of intelligence. The school teacher may be an example of the first type, and the secretary or stenographer of the second type. The professor lives in a universe of theories bounded by the buildings that face his university campus. The secretary or stenographer is constantly dealing in the thoughts of others, a person of responsibility but still a vicarious participant in the practice of thinking.

The Mercurial mind, developing beyond the estate of secretary or stenographer, naturally inclines toward intellectual pursuits, drawn to such occupations as editor, journalist or correspondent, essayist or even novelist or dramatist. In these careers, however, he must train himself against superficial treatment of his material. The writer who takes nothing seriously and whose veracity is far from unimpeachable typifies another danger in the development of the Gemini temperament.

Two unusual examples of the Gemini type in the field of letters are Dante and Bernard Shaw. Dante wrote his *Inferno* so that he could show in luminous verbiage all his enemies roasting in the pits of perdition. The Shavian humor has about it the bite of shallowness. It is not the deep laughter of the gods who understand all, but the shallow titillating laughter of mortals who understand not even themselves.

It is from the ranks of the neo-intellectuals that we develop our parlor socialists, our "modernists" in poetry and letters, and those arm-chair anarchists who have theoretical explanations for every circumstance of living.

The Mercurial person must take careful stock of himself and make sure that he contributes nothing to the inanities of the day.

We are forced to remind the reader that Gemini is unusually conspicuous in the annals of certain types of crime. In the lower scale, Gemini, ruling the fingers, bestows a certain lightness upon them, resulting in pickpockets and forgers. Truthfulness in particular is difficult to Gemini people. They do not necessarily intend to say anything that is really wrong, but with the general common sign dislike to assume unpleasant responsibility or to acknowledge faults, there is a tendency to try and fib one's way out of uncomfortable situations.

On the good side of the ledger we can sum up the virtues of the Gemini temperament thus: Quick, active, alert mentality, versatile, adjustable, non-combative, generous, humorous, and moderately temperate; interested in self-improvement, usually well read, good conversationalists and linguists, and even good performers on the piano or violin. Among the men there is sometimes a mechanical trend, turning interest to the automotive or airplane industries. There is an inventive streak, some restlessness and love of travel.

Gemini men are reasonably fortunate in marriage and should marry women of a Venus or Jupiter temperament. Gemini women are not always so fortunate, and must cultivate a tendency against drabness and lack of color in personality. The Gemini temperament being Mercurial, reflects the peculiar quality of Mercury which takes on the attitudes and appearance of whatever other sign or planet is most prominent in the nativity. The "double" Gemini person is usually not demonstrative in matters of affection, and is somewhat critical of those with whom he comes in contact.

The health of the Gemini is not robust, generally the greatest point of weakness being the lungs and bronchial tubes. This sign is also subject to nervous disorders and these persons must fortify themselves against worry and nervous tension.

The general course of the Gemini person should be directed toward deepening and rounding out the life with experience, seeking completeness in whatever branch of learning or pursuit the native is engaged.

The religious instincts are not usually highly developed, but the Gemini native, carefully avoiding all intensely emotional forms of religion, should develop its more philosophical aspects. The Gemini thinker is apt to pass through the experience of agnosticism and atheism. He must also avoid one peculiar fault that is part of his subjective make-up. He must not be overwhelmed by the opinions of others or accept too much of the authority of persons he respects. The Gemini mind can be awed into a state of acceptance and is greatly impressed by persons who claim to be authorities on various subjects. It is a good plan to remember the words of Buddha when he said: "I will accept nothing as truth regardless of authority, unless I can prove it in myself."

♍

VIRGO

(Those born August 23—September 22)

Virgo is also a sign under the rulership of Mercury, but the influence of this intellectual planet is less obvious and pronounced than in Gemini. Virgo people are peculiarly associated with the problem of responsibility. From the standpoint of happiness in this world, Virgo is not a particularly choice sign to be born under. But if we measure Virgo people we will discover that they accomplish a great deal and have lives rich in experience and laden with good deeds.

(53)

The keyword of the sign of Virgo is service —persons born under the sign are predestined to some form or kind of service. On the lower scale of development servitude is evident, but with the more highly advanced types service takes on complicated aspects in a larger theatre of action. Many Virgo persons go into professions which involve personal service or ministration, such as medicine or nursing. In the healing arts they are apt to be progressive and the sign produces naturopaths, chiropractors, mental and faith healers. Dependable in financial matters, the Virgo native is frequently chosen as guardian, trustee, administrator or executor, and can be expected to fulfill such duties with the most scrupulous care.

The less evolved types of Virgo persons have a somewhat distressful tendency to loquaciousness. They sort of rattle along, perpetuating unimportant conversations and indulging in endless repetition and annoying dissection of details. All Virgos do not have this proclivity, but where it exists it frequently leads to unintentional but disastrous gossiping.

Virgo people need travel and the broadening influence of wide reading and interesting acquaintances. They need to get their minds off themselves and their personal affairs and to take healthy interest in the larger concerns of life and society. They must also avoid being excessively egocentric, and should be particularly watchful that their conversation and thinking is not too greatly focussed upon their own ideas and opinions.

Virgo mothers have a constant tendency to spoil their children, combining indulgence and overshadowing in an often disastrous chemistry. Failing in other relationships in life, the Virgo mother may cling desperately to her children, seeking in them the only outlet to a thwarted emotional life. Under such conditions the solution is the development of satisfying mental interests. The study of metaphysics is most appropriate to these persons whose minds are usually capable of clear and constructive thinking, once proper interests have been established. Virgo women are better executives than Virgo men, and these women are frequently forced into public life as the support or protector of a family. Having assumed the duties of a man in relationship to her own family, it is difficult for her to encompass an adequate domestic attitude. She is therefore likely to draw to herself in the marriage relation a negative man and retain her own position as head of the family.

The Virgo man is usually of intermediate bodily size, industrious, suited to clerical, office and secretarial work, frequently has musical talent, and is somewhat of a disciplinarian in his home. He is serious and resourceful, but unless he watches his personal psychology may become nagging and old-maidish. I have observed that Virgo men frequently engage in promotional enterprises, are over-trusting in investments, but are blessed with a considerable amount of self-assurance, and usually come to positions of security and responsibility in their communities. The Virgo man is a detail thinker and does not succeed well in positions where he has to contact or work with a wide diversity of temperaments.

All Virgo people have a tendency to be very critical of others and to magnify the importance of details, thus losing sight of prime issues. They need to watch for blind spots in their reasoning and train themselves to broad and tolerant viewpoints. They need education and if it is denied them in early life should seek it in later years. Broadened in understanding, their ever quick sympathies can make them among the most useful and helpful of people.

↗

SAGITTARIUS

(Those born November 23—December 21)

The Sagittarian, being ruled by the expansive, indulgent planet Jupiter, has a psychology of life very different from the preceding Mercurial types. The common sign quality here manifests itself through easygoing and somewhat irresponsible tendencies. It is hard for the Sagittarian to take life profoundly. Usually blessed with a pleasing personality and a considerable personal magnetism, he tries to bluff his way to success, assiduously avoiding hard work and any form of intense mental or physical activity.

Sagittarians are versatile and the sign equips those born under it for a wide variety of arts, crafts or trades. Through choice or destiny the Sagittarian is frequently found in public life; in fact he flourishes best in an atmosphere of adulation and recognition. A pleasing, jovial personality and a well developed dramatic sense fit him for promotion and salesmanship. His naturally expansive ideas, supported by powerful enthusiasm, make him valuable in the development and expansion of various business enterprises. The professions strongly appeal to him and the sign

(57)

produces a heavy percentage of lawyers, politicians, theologians and physicians. The Sagittarian is eloquent and genial, possessing the qualities of diplomacy and friendliness, thus inducing popularity and public confidence.

The danger from the temperament arises in the comparative ease with which the Sagittarian can get along in the world. Usually somewhat lacking in will power and easily flattered, the unwary Sagittarian may wake up some day to find that he has been the tool for ulterior motives of others. There is a strong element of intemperance and an inordinate development of the appetites common to this sign, and the gambling instinct is seldom absent. The race track devotee, the stock market speculator, and thousands of other easy-believers who expect wealth and happiness to come without effort, or who chance everything on a throw of the dice, are exhibiting uncontrolled Sagittarian impulses. The hail-fellow-well-met has a hazardous future, and this sign is generally improvident. In all, the Sagittarian is juvenile, and unless he works very hard on himself has great difficulty in arriving at a mature state of reflection.

As already suggested, the sign of Sagittarius is highly diversified, and the superior types of all signs exhibit the virtues rather than the vices of their celestial rulers. Deepened and refined by self-discipline and education, the Sagittarian develops a fine sense of justice and a benign and compassionate attitude toward humanity, and is therefore the natural philanthropist. He admires education, has a well developed sense of veneration, is somewhat traditional, and tends to acceptance of old opinions and beliefs. He is not an innovationist in his personal life, his personal code being frequently far more conservative than his actions.

Sagittarius is the sign of hobbies. Many Sagittarians indulge in various sports, and if other signs in the personal horoscope give agreement, have a flair for athletics and horsemanship. Many Sagittarians are sickly in childhood and are subject to serious health problems throughout life. They consequently read considerably and in advancing years are often collectors or connoisseurs of art or patrons of the sciences, their benevolences usually going in the direction of culture or education.

The Sagittarian woman is not usually blessed with great physical beauty, as the sign tends to large bones and a lanky or angular appearance, often giving a long face or prominent teeth. The women are active, frequently athletic, and often engage in philanthropy or educational enterprises. They are not very domestic, but are charming and pleasant companions.

Sagittarian men often marry women interested in education or schools, or who have come up through business experience. Both Sagittarian men and women have usually a jovial disposition, with an undercurrent of melancholy and considerable timidity underneath what seems to be a strong or brilliant personality.

Deepened by experience and perfected through intelligent effort, the Sagittarian is the true philosopher of the zodiac, but the achievement of the philosophical life is not easy. Until they find themselves, Sagittarians are empty and lonely. They bestow their affections generously but somewhat impersonally, seeking first companionship from those with whom they associate themselves. Sagittarians are frequently sought for advice and guidance because of a certain strength of personality which inspires confidence and respect from others.

Though apparently robust, they share the general weakness of common sign constitutions, being subject to ailments of the circulation and nerves. This sign is sometimes subject to paralysis and accidents, especially to the legs.

Jupiter, the ruler of the sign, often bestows wealth and dignity, and if they administer their affairs with reasonable intelligence, Sagittarians will find that they are oddly protected as to their needs. The sign bestows security and the capacity to devote life to mental pursuits. It is one of the signs of the zodiac which demands of those born under it a greater integrity and dedication to ideals and principles.

♓

PISCES

(Those born February 19—March 20)

Pisces is the last of the common signs and rulership over it is shared by Jupiter and Neptune. The Neptunian element of fatalism is the dominant force in the lives of most Piscean people. Neptune is a strange planet, and those born under its dominion live unusual lives, moved by irresistible factors to mysterious ends.

Health is nearly always a problem to the Piscean. The constitution is not strong and the resistance to disease usually low. Glandular ailments are the most common, manifesting in unbalanced weight and general lassitude. The Pisces native may feel that he was born tired, and from early life is burdened with problems and responsibilities. The childhood may be unhappy and timidity affects the decisions upon which the success of life depends. The Piscean is susceptible to colds due to low resistance, and his whole bodily economy lacks tone and temper. He dislikes exercise and exertion, suffers with his feet, and seldom stands up when it is possible for him to sit down. He is physically uncomfortable for the greater part of his life. He is also subject to ailments of the sensory perceptions, especially the ears and eyes.

The physical background is bound to influence the mental viewpoint, bestowing an early sense of seriousness and responsibility. The childhood home is likely to be unhappy, stepparents are often indicated, or the native is out of harmony with his parental environment. Thrust upon his own resources early, he finds his life rendered hazardous by lack of decision. He is evasive in temperament, not forceful, and if he falls in with undesirable associates is easily influenced to his own detriment. Being somewhat negative in his own nature the Piscean is greatly influenced by his environment, is supersensitive to criticism, and needs gentle, sympathetic handling to bring out the best side of his nature. Naturally sensitive and noncombative, he is easily hurt, is overly shy and therefore emotionally introverted.

Under all the weakness, however, there is an unsuspected strength of character, an intense courage of conviction, even to the point of martyrdom. The sign is a strange combination of strength and weakness, difficult to understand, and apt not to be fully appreciated in a generation conscious only of the obvious.

The Piscean is not fitted for physical labor or for ordinary routine work, and succeeds best in humanitarian or educational pursuits. Working under the stimulus of inspiration or dedication, the Piscean can accomplish an incredible amount of constructive work. The more highly evolved Pisceans are fitted for occult and metaphysical pursuits and for medicine or the ministry. The less evolved types may follow the sea or engage in occupations which bring them extensive periods of solitude. They are also conspicuous in the fields of social and political reform, in social service work, and in lines of endeavor where they minister to the physical, mental or emotional needs of humanity. The negative side of the Pisces nature results in psychic sensitiveness, equipment of the natural medium, the clairvoyant or telepathist. This sensitiveness makes the Piscean keenly aware of the thoughts and feelings of the people around him and his own peace of mind is easily disrupted by the reactions of friends, relatives and associates. The keynote of the sign is sensitivity, leading almost inevitably to introversion.

Like the Virgo people, the Pisces natives are placed in positions of responsibility and trust. They are born worriers, with the unfortunate tendency to anticipate the worst. Only with the assistance of more positively minded associates, and stimulated to a high degree of self-discipline can the Piscean overcome natal indecisions, and the unworthy emotion of self-pity.

The Piscean must set seriously to work upon his own life, starting probably with the health angle. Having overcome the infirmities of the flesh as much as possible, he will find a great change in his whole life. The lack of physical energy is the real key to most of his mental and emotional indecisions. The sign is not generally long-lived, but being more or less constantly ailing the system becomes accustomed to functioning inadequately. As a result suddenly or serious illness is unlikely and the Piscean "enjoys" his bad health for a reasonable span of years.

Given motive or purpose and dedicated to high resolve, the Piscean rises to emergency and can become truly great. Rich in sympathy and compassion; deep in understanding; tolerant and liberal; endowed with strong intuitional and rational powers; the highly evolved Piscean is a deeply spiritual and intensely practical person. This sign produces religious and social leaders and reformers, mystics, seers and sages.

CPSIA information can be obtained
at www.ICGtesting.com
Printed in the USA
LVHW031809100223
739202LV00003B/499